# DEDICATION

This book is dedicated with love and respect to Mary, Tommy, and Jenni.

ACKNOWLEDGMENTS

Our appreciation goes to everyone who helped with this edition of Reaching Out to Today's Kids. Special thanks go to Rebecca Williamson for getting the ball rolling, Milburn Taylor for his delightful illustrations, and all of our friends who are parents and educators. Kathy is especially grateful to Susie, whose collaboration on this new edition has added to its usefulness and appeal.

ABOUT THE AUTHORS

Kathleen McConnell is an educational consultant for school districts and community service providers. She holds an undergraduate degree and a masters in education from the University of Delaware and a Ph.D. from the University of Texas at Austin. The mother of a son and daughter, Kathy writes from experience as both a parent and an educator. Her work with children who have emotional disturbances/behavior disorders focuses on practical solutions to problems. Kathy's recent interests include support for general educators as they take on the challenges of diverse, interesting, and active classrooms.

Susie Kelly Flatau is an author and teacher of creative writing, as well as a speaker, book editor, and freelance writer. Susie's books *Counter Culture Texas* and *From My Mother's Hands* are well known in Texas and reflect her interest in preserving our family and community legacies. She is co-editor of *Red Boots & Attitude* (a collection of works by notable Texas women writers), slated for a February 2002 release. Susie's fiction appears in *New Texas 2000*. For many years Susie was a secondary English teacher, recognized by her peers and supervisors for her enthusiasm, creativity, and positive spirit.

CONTENTS

INTRODUCTION

When the first edition of this book was written almost eight years ago, we were both parents of teenagers. We were trying to deal with our own children while also offering support and suggestions to other parents and teachers. As any of you who are parents or teachers know, adolescents and youth in our country today face significant problems. Their problems are reflected in the statistics and reports you read daily in the newspaper and see on television. Topics like school violence; drug and alcohol abuse; aggressive and dangerous acting-out behaviors; depression and suicide; alienation from friends, families, and school; high dropout rates; and kids in conflict with society's values are all reminders to us of how difficult it is to grow up in today's world. Parents and educators today, as they were eight years ago, are still concerned about these problems and are still looking for ways to connect with today's kids, whether their own children or their students at school.

Our experiences as teachers and teacher educators have provided us with some insight into ways in which teachers can work effectively with troubled youth. Because we are also parents, we have some tips that other parents might find useful. As most parents know, it is one thing for a teacher to try a strategy with an adolescent or child and quite another for a parent to successfully implement a similar plan. We are providing information in this edition of the book that was not as readily available eight years ago. In addition to the suggestions and ideas, each chapter now includes additional references and resources that we believe you will find helpful. At the request of some of our readers, we have also included space for readers to reflect and record their own impressions, so that the book can be used as a journal or planner. We hope that these changes will make it even easier to find support and assistance. We recognize that solutions for difficult problems are not quick, easy, or foolproof. All we can do is try. In the first edition of the book, we articulated three principles for working with young people. While many things have changed in the last eight years, our commitment to these principles has not. In working with youth, we continue to believe that

1. Change is possible.

2. In the long run, positive approaches work better than negative ones.

3. Things can get better.

We are pleased to share our ideas with you and hope that you enjoy them.

IDEA 1 — MAKE A CONNECTION

"Give kids a chance to speak their minds."

—Salvador, 12

SMILE. Sometimes we forget that our body language, facial expressions, and tone of voice say as much as our words. If it has been a while since you and your student or child had an easy, friendly conversation, you may want to start with a smile. It can tell them how much you care and that you are willing to hang in there with them.

START TO TALK. When we find ourselves in patterns of behavior that involve hurt feelings, anger, resentment, and fear, we sometimes stop talking to each other. We may even respond by yelling. Being the first to initiate a friendly conversation may be difficult, but if you start small, it can work. Nonthreatening statements, compliments, or offers of assistance are ways to generate friendly conversations. For example:

☼ **"It's a nice day today. Are you doing anything special after school?"**

☼ **"Would you like to go to the store with me?"**

☼ **"That shirt looks good on you."**

☼ **"The Spurs won the game last night. They're really hot!"**

☼ **"Does anybody want to help me cook hamburgers for dinner?"**

HELP THEM, EVEN WHEN THEY DON'T ASK FOR IT. Sometimes children want to do difficult things by themselves, and you should let them. Other times, they need your help and just will not ask. When teachers and parents offer to help youngsters with small things, it can tell them you still care. For example:

☼ Find out if they need help with their homework.

☼ Ask if you could fix them a snack after they get home from work.

☼ Make them a haircut appointment and take them without being asked. (Only do this one if you are sure it will be appreciated.)

☼ Ask if they have the supplies they need to finish a project or to participate in an activity.

GIVE THEM A PAT ON THE BACK OR A HUG. Once you have worked through the more difficult issue of initiating a friendly exchange, you may want to give your child a pat on the back or a hug. We realize that lawsuits are prominent in today's society, and we are not implying that suggestive or inappropriate touches be used with students. But you might be surprised how very effective a handshake, high five, wink, or nod can be as positive reinforcement. Often, when your children make you feel the least like hugging them is when they need it the most.

"We need to make sure that no boy or girl in America is growing up without having in his or her life the presence of a responsible, caring adult. Where else does a child learn how to behave? Where else does a child learn the experience of the past, the totems and traditions of the past? Where else does a child look for the proper examples except from responsible, caring, loving adults in his or her life."

—General Colin L. Powell, United States Army (retired)
Secretary of State (2001-)

America's Promise—The Alliance for Youth
http://63.98.236.133/FivePromises/CaringAdults.cfm

MY REFLECTIONS

_____

_____

_____

_____

_____

_____

_____

_____

_____

_____

_____

_____

_____

WEBSITES/RESOURCES

- www.primenet.com/~bdi/ (Behavioral-Developmental Initiatives)
- www.FamilyEducation.com (Learning Network)
- www.familycares.org (Family Cares)

REFERENCES

Chemofsky, Barbara. *Change your child's behavior by changing yours.* Crown, 1995.

Windell, James. *6 Steps to an emotionally intelligent teenager: Teaching social skills to your teen.* Wiley & Sons, 1999.

Wolf, Anthony E. *Get out of my life, but first could you drive me & Cheryl to the mall?: A parent's guide to the new teenager.* Farrar, Straus & Giroux, 1991.

NOTES TO MYSELF

_____

_____

_____

_____

_____

_____

_____

_____

_____

_____

_____

_____

_____

IDEA 2 RECOGNIZE DEEPER FEELINGS

"When you give teens RESPECT, they act more RESPONSIBLE."

—Sheila, 16

PUT YOURSELF IN HIS OR HER PLACE. When you get into a cycle of negative behavior with children or adolescents, it is difficult to think of them as anything other than the enemy. It may be helpful to remember how you felt when you were their age. The ability to empathize with others is an important skill for adults and young people to develop and use. When you put yourself in others' positions, it is easier to understand why they do what they do. Some ways to do this with the young person in your life:

☼ If you are the parent, remember when the child was a baby. Get out those baby pictures and try to call up those protective, loving feelings that you had then.

☼ If you are a teacher, try to imagine how your students feel when they are alone—how hurt, lonely, or inadequate they might feel when they're alone thinking at night.

☼ Remember that people who are happy do not fight, call names, pout, or push their friends away. When they act out, they probably are very unhappy.

EMPATHIZE AND RELATE. Once you are able to empathize and see the young person's point of view, recognize how she or he must be feeling. When people are feeling good about themselves, they don't need to be confrontational, to prove themselves to others, or to say and do hurtful things. When you see a student being mean to other children or withdrawing from social contacts, it is likely that he or she is unhappy or in pain. This occurs often among children who have been physically or sexually abused, but children today have many sources of stress. Their acting out is often in response to unhappiness or negative emotions.

READ BETWEEN THE LINES. Adolescents and youth, like many adults, do not always know what they are feeling. What they say is not necessarily what they really mean. Some young men and women today find it difficult to ask for help, express affection, accept a compliment, or tell someone when they are upset. Most of us really want to be cared for by those we know and love. Children may not tell parents and teachers that they want their approval or attention, but usually they do. Almost all of us have a need to feel connected to someone. Unfortunately, many young people today get those feelings from negative peer groups like gangs, instead of from families and classmates. The key is to assume that you are important to the young person no matter what he or she says.

"It's easy to get very stressed out. I don't think there are many people who haven't at least sometime in their life thought. 'You know, wouldn't it be easier if I went over to that tall building and did a nice jump?' But that's an escape. If you get into the habit of running away, you're never going to have the chance to face reality. Life is a challenge for everyone, but the most important thing is to start enjoying challenges."

—Rod Tranum
www.lifesplaybook.com

MY REFLECTIONS

"Chill! Five Steps to Burnout Prevention" Rod Tranum

Source: The Prevention Index 1993, *Prevention Magazine*, published by Rodale Press

WEBSITES/RESOURCES

- www.angermgmt.com (Anger Management)
- www.lifesplaybook.com (Life's Playbook Program)
- www.parentsworld.com (Single Parents World)

REFERENCES

Covey, Sean. *The 7 habits of highly effective teens: The ultimate teenage success guide.* Simon & Schuster, 1998.

McGraw, Jay. *Life strategies for teens.* Simon & Schuster, 2000.

Riera, Michael, and Joseph DiPrisco. *Field guide to the American teenager: A parent's companion: Appreciate the teenager you live with.* Perseus Books Group, 2000.

NOTES TO MYSELF

IDEA 3 — SPEND TIME

"Adults shouldn't put so much pressure on their children. Maybe if they gave them time to relax for awhile, they would put their problems behind them."

—Kerry, 15

YOUNG PEOPLE NEED YOUR TIME. If you want to maintain good relationships, especially with your children or students, you have to spend time with them. There is no substitute for your attention. When you are with your children or students it gives you an opportunity to listen and talk to them. Seize all the chances you get to maintain contact with them:

- ☀ In the car on the way home
- ☀ At the grocery store
- ☀ Taking the dog for a walk
- ☀ In line at the bank

- ☀ At night before going to bed
- ☀ Before and after school
- ☀ In the hallways at school
- ☀ At sports events

You understand . . . don't you, Bowser?

Most important of all, have dinner together several times a week. This is a key to maintaining good communication.

LEARN TO LISTEN. Some children go through an entire day without having an adult really listen to them. Especially at school, one of the nicest things you can do for some students is to sit down and listen to them. Finding time to listen is especially difficult in secondary schools where teachers see as many as 100 students every day. Use time between classes, before school, and after school for those students having problems. You might be the only person they have who will listen to them. For parents, it is especially important to stop talking to and at your children so you can find out what they're thinking.

ASK QUESTIONS. Parents and teachers can find out a lot by listening, but when you're not sure of something or you'd like to know what's going on, ask. If you are just beginning to reestablish a relationship, make sure the questions are not too intrusive or challenging, but if you and the youth in question are able to relate fairly well already, ask some open-ended questions like:

- ☀ **"So what happened at school today?"**

- ☀ **"Can I help you with anything?"**

- ☀ **"Would you like to have lunch with me this weekend so we can talk?"**

- ☀ **"Wanna talk?"**

- ☀ **"How's the world treating you?"**

- ☀ **"Is everything going okay with your boyfriend [girlfriend]?"**

REACH OUT. Many children and youth are growing up in single-parent families—often with only their mothers. We are or have been single mothers and know how challenging the role can be. Lots of single moms and dads do a great job with their children, but it's usually very difficult for them because their economic situation requires that they work outside the home. If you are in one of the families with two parents and you feel comfortable about doing so, share your time and include the kids you know from single-parent families in some activities. Large numbers of young boys and girls in this country are growing up without both parents to guide them. While many grow up to be well-adjusted, successful adults, others struggle with feelings of abandonment and rejection. Often, the custodial parent is overwhelmed with responsibilities and just needs a little relief. Lend a hand if you can.

"One of the most important skills good listeners have is the ability to put themselves in the shoes of others or empathize with the speaker by attempting to understand his or her thoughts and feelings. As a parent try to mirror your children's feelings by repeating them."

—Carl Smith

"How Can Parents Model Good Listening Skills?" Carl Smith
www.focusas.com

MY REFLECTIONS

_____

_____

_____

_____

_____

_____

_____

_____

_____

_____

_____

_____

_____

_____

WEBSITES/RESOURCES

- www.focusas.com (Focus Adolescent Services)
- www.positiveparenting.com (Positive Parenting)
- www.familyresources.com (Family Resources)

REFERENCES

Faber, Adele, and Elaine Mazlish. *How to talk so kids will listen & listen so kids will talk.* Morrow, William & Co., 1999.

Nichols, Michael P. *The lost art of listening.* Guilford Publications, 1996.

Pipher Mary. *Shelter of each other: Rebuilding our families.* Random House, 1997.

NOTES TO MYSELF

IDEA 4 — BE CONSISTENT

"When I speak of encouragement, I do not mean a parent towering above their child, preaching on what they did wrong, nor do I relate to a parent lowering their standards in order to connect with that child and telling them their actions are accepted. The goal in encouraging someone is to help that person learn to self-apply encouragement. Encouragement involves the balancing between autonomy and belonging, and is simultaneously a realization of a person's strength and weaknesses."

—Linda, 15

STICK TO THE RULES. After weighing our experiences as parents and as teachers, we both believe that it is a lot easier to be a consistent teacher than a consistent parent. In part, this is because teachers have less of an emotional attachment to their students than to their own children. We also believe that our own children know us well and have learned how to get to us more quickly and more deeply. Also, when we're tired, frazzled, or trying to relax, we tend to let things slide. When deciding on rules, try to reflect what you really will and will not tolerate. Things that are important to you may not matter to someone else. But, no matter what your rules are for your home or classroom, stick to the rules you do make. To the extent possible, be consistent. Do what you say you are going to do—*every time*. Remember, too, that even if you don't always agree, some community and school-wide rules will also be needed and enforced. Teach your children to respect those as well.

BE SURE YOU EXPLAIN THE RULES CLEARLY. When you make rules, be sure that your students or children understand them. It is important to not make so many rules that they can't remember them and you can't enforce them. Also, it is not fair for you to change the rules in midstream. You can be sure that your students or children understand the rules by using some simple procedures:

- ☀ Ask them to restate (repeat) the rule back to you.

- ☀ Model (demonstrate) what you mean.

- ☀ Let them ask you questions ("What if I do this? Does this count? Is this what you mean?").

- ☀ Have them demonstrate for you.

- ☀ When a rule gets broken, give them a chance to explain why it happened, just in case of a misunderstanding.

BE CLEAR ABOUT CONSEQUENCES. With every system of rules, it is important to have clearly defined consequences. This means positive responses, like privileges, compliments, and other rewards, as well as consequences that are punitive, like restrictions on activities, reprimands, or denial of privileges. When applying consequences, follow these basic principles: Make the punishment fit the crime. Try not to overreact or underreact to transgressions. Be clear and consistent. Young people will try to test the limits of adults' tolerance, but once they know what is going to happen with some certainty, they often modify their behavior to fit the expectations. Again, while consistency can be difficult to achieve, it is worth the effort. Consistency is a key to changing children's behavior.

BE FLEXIBLE. Do not mistake consistency for rigidity. Exceptions, extenuating circumstances, and special situations no doubt will occur. If you never bend when you deal with adolescents and youth, you may find yourself in a serious no-win confrontation. In the long run, you need to be consistent. Consistency gives young people boundaries that they can respect. Consistency enables them to trust you, because they know that you really will do what you say you'll do. Flexibility shows them you're human.

"We must not only initially provide consistent consequences or rules to help our children, and then become more flexible without losing the boundaries, but we must also by our own actions reflect our ideals, our morals and values. The best form of teaching is by example."

—PageWise, Inc.

"Parenting technique: Consequences are teaching for structure."
°2001 by PageWise, Inc.
http://nm.essortment.com/parentingtechni_rqmo.htm

MY REFLECTIONS

_____

_____

_____

_____

_____

_____

_____

_____

_____

_____

_____

_____

_____

_____

WEBSITES/RESOURCES

- www.backincontrol.com (Back in Control)
- www.childparenting.about.com (About-The Human Internet)
- www.awareparenting.com (Aware Parenting Institute)

REFERENCES

Kelly, Kate. *The complete idiot's guide to parenting a teenager*. Alpha Books, 1996.

Tracy, F., and Louise Felton Tracy. *Grounded for life: Stop blowing your fuse and start communicating*. Parenting PR, 1994.

Windell, James. *8 Weeks to a well-behaved child*. Book News, 1995.

NOTES TO MYSELF

IDEA 5

LET THEM KNOW YOU'RE HUMAN

"When your kids turn about ten years old, tell them this and make sure they're listening: 'In life, it's not perfect, some things will go your way and some won't.' But, tell them to never forget that when things get bad, they can turn it around and make it good. And life goes on. . ."

—Annie, 17

TELL THEM THAT YOU HAVE HAD "ANOTHER LIFE." When you are a teacher, sometimes students don't understand that you are a real person with a life outside of school. I can recall an occasion when I was grocery shopping and saw one of my students. He seemed surprised to see me and couldn't stop staring. Finally, I asked him if anything was wrong. He replied, "You've got legs." It wasn't news to me, of course, but apparently he was shocked to see me not only in a totally different context, but also in shorts and sandals. It doesn't hurt to share some personal information about your family and your life at home with your students.

If you are a parent, it is also important to tell your children about the experiences you had at their age. Let them know that you had the same hopes and dreams they have and that you made some mistakes along the way. These shared experiences give you a basis for communication when they say, "You just don't understand!"

SHOW THEM PICTURES. One of our colleagues always gets oohs and aahs from the education majors when he shows them pictures from his days of playing in a rock band with shoulder-length hair. It's a nice reminder that people do change and that it is okay to try different things and dress in different ways. We always showed my younger students pictures of our own children so they knew that we understood a little bit about family life. We

also kept a photo album in the classroom, and the kids loved to look at themselves and see how they had changed over time. It's important for children and teenagers to have a sense of the continuity of life, so they can see past school and think about their future in the real world.

DEMONSTRATE A FULL RANGE OF EMOTIONS. We think it's healthy for young people to see adults experience lots of different feelings. We hope that we model constructive ways of dealing with emotions. But the truth is, many adults don't always handle things as well as they should. It is important to let your class or your children know that everyone gets upset and that sometimes you feel sad and other times you are angry. Unfortunately, most of us didn't grow up in homes with parents who modeled calm, well thought out expressions like these:

☼ **"Okay, Sally, I'm angry and I want you to watch what I do. I'm going to tell Dad what I'm angry about, then I'm going to go for a long walk. Later, I'll discuss the situation with him when I'm more in control."**

or

☼ **"I am crying because I had a bad day at work. One of my friends got upset with me, then I found out that my project had a big mistake in it, and I was late for a meeting. All in all, it was a lousy day. I'll be better after a good cry."**

Instead, many of us have learned effective ways of dealing with emotions through trial and error, help from counselors, or by watching what others do. Letting young people know that there are many different emotions and that it's normal to feel differently at different times is helpful to them. When you deal constructively and calmly with those feelings, it's even better.

"Parents trip up when it comes to showing genuine empathy. It's difficult to empathize when you're upset or angry or reeling from something your child has just said. Sometimes parents confuse empathy with encouragement."

—Dr. Paul Coleman

excerpt from How To Say It to Your Kids by Dr. Paul Coleman; in "Smart Talk: The Six Ways We Speak to Our Kids"
http://familyeducation.com/article/0,1120,1-23220-0-3,00.html

MY REFLECTIONS

WEBSITES/RESOURCES

- www.lifematters.com (LifeMatters)
- www.syndistar.com (Syndistar)
- www.tnpc.com (The National Parenting Center)

REFERENCES

Christopher, Doris. *Come to the table: A celebration of family life.* Warner Books, 1999.

Siegler, Ava L. *The essential guide to the new adolescence: How to raise an emotionally healthy teenager.* Dutton/Plume, 1998.

Steinberg, Laurence, and Ann Levine. *You and your adolescent: A parent's guide for ages 10 to 20.* HarperCollins, 1997.

NOTES TO MYSELF

IDEA 6

HELP THEM SEE THE RELATIONSHIP BETWEEN NOW AND LATER

"Face it, when you have a group of kids in your face or someone telling you how to be cool and fit in, it is hard if you do not have any standing ground."

—Sandy, 14

TELL THEM WHAT IS POSSIBLE. Research has shown that many students, including some from low socioeconomic backgrounds, often have trouble understanding the relationship between what they do and what they get. For lots of American children, the concerns of life are immediate: whether there will be heat at home and enough food for dinner or whether they will get medicine when they are sick. It can be very difficult for these young people to set goals that involve a long-term commitment, or to see the payoff for working hard and sticking with an activity or task whose rewards are not immediately apparent.

A student may feel that he or she doesn't really have any control over what happens; that fate or luck are more important than effort. Parents and teachers have a number of ways to let young people know that they, in fact, have some control over their own destiny. One teacher uses a Reminder Card. This bright index card reads:

> When I am 25 years old, I want to be working at a decent job and have money to spend for fun. To do this I MUST develop good work and study habits, learn social skills to get along with other people, and get a basic education.
>
> Looking at this reminder several times daily helps me realize that my everyday behavior at school and home affects my chances for success as an adult.

This teacher works with some very challenging 14- and 15-year olds, and although the Reminder Card is not his only helpful tool for students, it is one that his students enjoy and use often.

EXPOSE THEM TO POSITIVE ROLE MODELS. All of us are influenced by others in our lives. Youth are very impressionable, and many will copy the actions of those they admire. Good role models for young people show them that it is possible to achieve and succeed. We know that the role models who are most influential are those most like ourselves, so it is important that girls have female role models and minority students have role models from their own ethnic/racial background. If you are a teacher, you can invite business-men and businesswomen, community leaders, parents, and retirees to visit with your students. If you are a parent, point out to your children what accomplishments are possible and let them get to know people with a variety of interests and achievements. It is nice to let them know that while most of us will not end up millionaires, we can still find jobs we enjoy and have rela-tively comfortable, happy lives.

TEACH THEM THAT SUCCESS COMES IN MANY PACKAGES. One of the biggest favors you can do for young people is to help them get an appreciation of the many ways to measure accom-plishment. A family I know whose daughter is severely disabled has shown lots of my students how to value things other than money, academic achievement, or athletic prowess. Instead, they have learned to appreci-ate someone who can make you laugh or someone

Success Comes in Many Packages

who teaches you compassion for others. For young people, learning to value themselves just for who they are is sometimes very difficult.

"Our society is so caught up with winning we forget that most of the great men and women in history have, at one time or another, failed at something. Often repeatedly, and discouragingly. But each failure is nothing more than a brick in the wall that forms the foundation of our success. We can't forget that."

—Joe Romig

MY REFLECTIONS

_____

_____

_____

_____

_____

_____

_____

_____

_____

_____

_____

_____

_____

_____

WEBSITES/RESOURCES

- www.rolemodel.net (Role Models on the Web)
- www.learningnetwork.com (Learning Network)
- www.parentsoup.com (parent soup)

REFERENCES

Benson, Susan, and Edmund Benson. *Positive role models*. Arise Foundation, 1999.

Dosick, Wayne. *Golden rules: The ten ethical values parents need to teach their children*. Harper, 1998.

Damon, William. *Greater expectations: Overcoming the culture of indulgence in our homes and schools*. Free Press, 1996.

NOTES TO MYSELF

IDEA 7 — TEACH THEM SOME POSITIVE VALUES

"ULTIMATELY, THE SCULPTOR OF MY FUTURE HAS BEEN MY DECISIONS. As an eighth grader, every decision that I make can have long term effects on both my academic and social future. Many of my past decisions I have come to regret, but I must take these experiences and examine them. The decision maker and only the decision maker has the power and ability to carve their own future and determine the path that they may follow: success or failure."

—Garret, 14

HELP THEM BE A PART OF THE FAMILY OR CLASSROOM UNIT. Families come in all configurations these days. Many children grow up in homes with one parent instead of two or in households with extended-family members. No matter the structure of the family, life usually goes more smoothly if the family works together to get things done. This means that everyone in the family must do his or her part. Whether it is laundry, cooking, house cleaning, washing the car, walking the dog, or emptying the trash, there are always chores to be done. It is important that the adults in a family not do all of the work themselves. If they do, they are depriving their children of the chance to learn what is involved in family life and to take some healthy responsibility for their share of the work. As at home, school is a place where students should be given some responsibilities in their classes, so that they understand that they have an important role as part of the group. When they depend on each other to get a job done, they learn to value each other and to cooperate. Give the young people in your life some responsibilities and then hold them accountable.

STRUCTURE THE TASKS. It seems that some people are naturally very organized. Structure, organization, and attention to detail come easily to them. Others find it more difficult to organize an environment. When dealing with young people, it is important to follow through after you have asked for their help. If you are one of those people who have a problem being consistent about expectations around the house or the classroom, here are some ideas that might work for you. Some are old stand-bys and some are a little more creative. The important thing is to use a system you feel comfortable with so that you are likely to continue to use it:

☀ Make a chart with names down the left hand side of the paper and chores across the top. Check off each child as he or she finishes a task.

☀ To alternate turns with one specific chore, write the names on a vertical list, in alternating order. Each day, after Chad takes his turn washing the dishes, he crosses off his name. Mandy's name is next, so she knows it's her turn to wash dishes the next day, then Stacy, and so on.

☀ Get a rack like one for hanging keys. Use plastic, wood, or stiff paper to make a circle with each child's name on it. Make one side green and the other red. Before the chore is done, the red side faces out. After the child completes a chore, she reverses the sign so the green shows, indicating she can now go somewhere because her chores are completed.

☀ Give out poker chips, coupons, or raffle tickets for completed tasks. Children can trade them in for money, pizzas, video rentals, or ice cream. Students can also earn free "100s" or skip a homework assignment. Each token earned is worth a set amount toward each goody.

☀ Let the children choose their chores, and alternate who chooses first. If you let young people have choices and take some control over what happens to them, they feel that they have some power.

ARRANGE THINGS SO THAT YOUNG PEOPLE HAVE TO WORK TOGETHER. In cooperative learning groups in school, it is important to structure things so that group members depend on each other and no one can finish the task without the help and cooperation of the other members of the group. This can be accomplished in several ways. For example, if the students in the class are creating a radio show about the Trojan Wars, the teacher would require that all four members of the group have a speaking part, that each group member write part of the text, and that each submit a list of what every person contributed, complete with signatures.

At home, many tasks can be structured for interactive participation, like preparing dinner (with each person completing one part of the meal) or washing the car (with one person squirting the hose, one person washing, and another person drying). Adults often complain that young people don't know how to work in groups effectively. Considering that they are rarely expected or required to work in groups at home or at school, it should not be surprising. We depend heavily on individual assignments and too often ask for individual efforts. Working together is fun, accomplishes more, and can have more interesting results.

HAVE SOME FUN TOGETHER. Another important part of family life is sharing laughter and fun. There are lots of young people whose parents are successful in their jobs and who can provide their children with unlimited material possessions. These same parents may be so busy that their children almost never get to spend time with them. Rarely do these families take the time to do things together. Many people believe that children whose families have money do not have problems. Unfortunately, young people from all backgrounds have stress in their lives, including parents who abuse alcohol or drugs, parents who consistently face financial stress, or parents who don't stop to get to know their families. Stop working and take the time to have some fun together. Laugh with each other at home and at school.

"Now more than ever we must take a good look at what we are teaching our children by the way we treat them. Controlling their behavior is simply not enough. We must help them become decision makers and critical thinkers. We must help them feel that they can contribute to society, and we must enhance their joy for learning."

—Richard Curwin and Allen Mendler

Discipline with Dignity by Richard Curwin and Allen Mendler
http://familyeducation.com/article/0,1120,1-7140,00.html

MY REFLECTIONS

WEBSITES/RESOURCES

- www.abcparenting.com (ABC's of Parenting)
- www.naturalchild.org (The Natural Child Project)
- www.cyh.com (Child and Youth Health)

REFERENCES

Berger, Elizabeth. *Raising children with character: Parents, trust, and the development of personal integrity.* Jason Aranson, 1999.

Covey, Stephen R. *The 7 habits family collection: Building a beautiful family culture in a turbulent world.* Franklin Covey, 1998.

Josephson, Michael S., and Wes Hanson (eds.). *The power of character.* Jossey-Bass, 1998.

NOTES TO MYSELF

IDEA 8

MAINTAIN HIGH EXPECTATIONS

"Go out and make the best out of what you have. Do what you want to get to where you want to be. Use the responsibility that is stored up inside and earn independence by easing into it one step at a time."

—Terri, 14

DON'T BE AFRAID TO TELL THEM WHEN THEY'RE OUT OF LINE. In working with students who are having emotional or behavioral problems, it is very important for parents and teachers to work together to maintain consistently high expectations. If you are the parent or teacher of a young person who is rude, disrespectful, or defiant, it is important that you not ignore these behaviors. When you allow such behavior, you are conveying the message that it is permissible and will be tolerated. However, in our larger society, employers and people we meet are not going to allow this type of acting out. The young person who is disrespectful and confrontational on the job will soon be unemployed. The young person who is consistently rude or hostile will not be able to maintain friendships and close personal relationships. Start teaching acceptable social behavior when students are young. Talk and act respectfully to your children or students and insist that they do the same to you.

LET THEM KNOW THEY ARE CAPABLE. Praise, praise, praise! When young people do something nice, compliment them. Let them know that you noticed and that you are impressed. It is a sad commentary on our society that many children do not know how to accept compliments or praise well. Unfortunately, it is because many of them have not had much experience.

There are millions of ways to show your approval and appreciation and to let young people know that you're proud of them:

☀ **"It was nice of you to unload the dishwasher. Thanks."**
"The phone call to your grandmother was sweet. You're really a great grandson."

☀ **"Way to go! The grade you got on that test was super!"**
"Thanks for helping me with the groceries. I'm really tired and I appreciate the help."

☀ **"You are really growing up to be a sensitive young lady. I'm very proud of you."**

EXPECT THE BEST. In school, as in family life, kids act differently in different situations and with different individuals. Remember when you were in high school? There were some classes in which everyone was wild, disrespectful, or uncooperative; those same students would be calm, respectful, and cooperative in a different class. Young people soon know exactly what is expected of them and they live up or down to those expectations. Do them a favor—expect that they can give you their best.

GIVE THEM OPPORTUNITIES TO BE TRUSTED. Getting started with trust can be very difficult. Start small. Entrust your children or students with a small task, wait for them to come through, then lavish them with praise. Tell them how proud you are of them and how nice it is to be able to trust them. Some little ways to get started include:

※ If your child can drive, let him take responsibility for something you usually do yourself, like grocery shopping, mailing a package, or getting the oil changed in the car. Make it a task that's not drudgery.

※ Don't always tell her what to do. Give her some choices about bedtime, telephone time, or curfew. The key here is to talk things over first. Ask her what she thinks would be fair, then negotiate.

※ In school, let the problem student help you. Give him or her some responsibility for recording grades, watering plants, conveying messages to the office, or keeping track of homework assignments. Find something he's good at, like the computer or art for a bulletin board.

※ Put the older child in charge of a younger child. Some of the most effective programs I've seen schools try are those using older, at-risk children to tutor, read aloud, or draw with younger children. It seems to bring out the best in them.

"Children are not your peers. They haven't the right—as do adults in contract disputes—to break off negotiations. Parents have the final say. Still, your children benefit when you hear them out, understand their reasons for wanting something, and sometimes negotiate an agreement with them."

—Dr. Paul Coleman

"Smart Talk: The Six Ways We Speak to Our Kids"; excerpted from How To Say it to Your Kids by Dr. Paul Coleman
http://familyeducation.com/article/0,1120,1-23220-0-4,00.html

MY REFLECTIONS

_____

_____

_____

_____

_____

_____

_____

_____

_____

_____

_____

_____

_____

_____

WEBSITES/RESOURCES

- www.parentsplace.com (Parents Place)
- www.hopewellpublishing.com (Hopewell Publishing)
- www.dadmag.com (DADMAG)

REFERENCES

Bluestein, Jane. *Parents, teens and boundaries: How to draw the line.* Health Communications, 1993.

Jim, Fay. *Parenting teens with love & logic: Preparing adolescents for responsible adulthood.* Navpress, 1993.

Kvols, Kathryn J. *Redirecting children's behavior.* Parenting Press, 1997.

NOTES TO MYSELF

IDEA 9 · TEACH THEM TO SOLVE PROBLEMS

"This is the chance you take with life. It is an ever changing scenario that has its many highs and lows. But yet, you still have great expectations and all you can hope is that you can accomplish them by yourself, because you can't expect anything from anyone else until you can go out and do it for yourself."

—Tina, 17

INTRODUCE A PROBLEM-SOLVING MODEL. We sometimes make assumptions about what young people have been taught to do. For example, if you are a teacher and you encounter a student who constantly interrupts conversations, you may assume that he or she is rude and has bad manners. However, if this same student has never been taught to wait to speak until another person is finished, or to say, "Excuse me for interrupting, but . . . ," then it is unfair and counterproductive to reprimand and chastise him or her. The better course of action would be to explain why it is best not to interrupt others, then model the correct way to take turns when speaking and how to interrupt politely when it is necessary to do so.

Likewise, students who never have been taught strategies for solving problems probably will not be too good at it until they are taught. Scolding or yelling will not teach them effective problem-solving methods. Role playing, modeling, direct instruction, and cooperative games are just some of the proven strategies that can help young people learn to solve problems. The five-step approach is simple and can be used in many different situations:

1. **Identify the problem.**

2. **Think of three possible solutions.**

3. **Think of advantages and disadvantages of each solution.**

4. **Choose the best alternative.**

5. **Remember if this choice doesn't work out, you can try something else.**

Children Learn From Both Good and Bad Role Models

HELP THEM LEARN TO MANAGE THEIR STRESS. People are most likely to act impulsively and make poor choices when they are tired, worried, nervous, angry, frustrated, or otherwise stressed. Contrary to what many adults might think, children today are subject to a great deal of stress.

Many children live in families that face problems of drug and alcohol abuse, poverty, unemployment, or other economic uncertainties. Children must also deal with pressures to do well academically, internal pressure to "be perfect," part-time jobs and extracurricular activities that require large amounts of time, pressures from peers to engage in sexual activity, and the day in and day out realities of trying to figure out who they are and how to become the kind of adults they want to be. Still other young people are homeless, incarcerated, or in rehabilitation facilities or hospitals.

Teachers, parents, and young people should all learn some stress reduction activities that work for them. Here are some suggestions:

- ☀ Taking a walk during lunch time
- ☀ Talking to a friend
- ☀ Crying in the shower
- ☀ Going for a long jog or run
- ☀ Listening to music
- ☀ Playing basketball
- ☀ Writing in a journal
- ☀ Laughing
- ☀ Going to a movie alone
- ☀ Taking a nap
- ☀ Writing a letter or description of what's going on
- ☀ Being alone
- ☀ Soaking in a hot bath
- ☀ Taking the dog for a walk and talking to him or her
- ☀ Cleaning up the house or yard
- ☀ Cooking something

HELP THEM KEEP THINGS IN PERSPECTIVE. Parents and teachers who overreact and panic when things go wrong are poor models for young people who are learning how to handle stress and pressure. It is not always possible to stay calm and thoughtful, but it helps to try. If you find yourself under a lot of stress, try to keep things in perspective. It is helpful to remember Reinhold Niebuhr's prayer: "Grant me the serenity to accept the things I cannot change, the courage to change those things I can, and the wisdom to know the difference." When things go wrong for our young people, help them to see that most times things can be fixed. When they see negative events as catastrophic, talk them through some solutions:

☀ **"Would you like to talk to me about what's going on? I'll be glad to listen and only give advice if you ask for it."**

☀ **"What are some possible solutions?"**

☀ **"You know, I think if we work together, we'll be able to solve this problem."**

☀ **"I've got some ideas. Here are two or three different ways we could handle this. Let's figure out which one would work."**

☀ **"Now, don't do anything drastic. I'll bet there's an answer."**

☀ **"Before you call or go see your friend, why don't you wait an hour or so?"**

"Listening respectfully to children—hearing their experience of events and interactions—is one very important way to give them your support. Remember to listen before offering advice."

—Family Education

"When Your Child Is Being Teased"
http://familyeducation.com/article/0,1120,20-5643-1,00.html

MY REFLECTIONS

_____

_____

_____

_____

_____

_____

_____

_____

_____

_____

_____

_____

_____

WEBSITES/RESOURCES

- www.parent.net (Parent News)
- www.kidtemp.com (The Temperament Learning Center)
- www.npin.org (National Parent Information Network)

REFERENCES

Carlson, Richard. *Don't sweat the small stuff*. Hyperion, 2000.

Dacey, John S., Lisa B. Fiore, George T. Ladd, and Lisa Fiore. *Your anxious child: How parents and teachers can relieve anxiety in children*. Jossey-Bass, 2000.

Riera, Michael. *Uncommon sense for parents with teenagers*. Celestial Arts, 1995.

NOTES TO MYSELF

IDEA 10
TEACH THEM TO HELP OTHERS

"I know that other opportunities to make a difference are out there, but they won't materialize in the dark cell I create for myself."

—Teresa, 16

LET THEM KNOW HOW GOOD IT FEELS TO HELP ANOTHER PERSON. All of us like to feel proud of ourselves. One way to feel good about our actions is to help someone who really needs it. Students who help others not only get the satisfaction of doing something worthwhile for someone else, they also get positive feedback from other people who appreciate and admire their actions.

Lists of volunteer opportunities often can be found in community newspapers, on church bulletin boards, or at various community service organizations. In many schools, classes have sponsored projects to help people who are homeless, to act as buddies for students with disabilities, to work on environmental cleanup activities, and to help refugees. The students involved have had many positive experiences and may have started a lifelong habit of community involvement. For students who feel alienated from their communities, acquiring a sense of belonging and membership is critical if they are to avoid joining gangs and engaging in other antisocial behavior. If you have a personal investment of time and energy in something, you may be less likely to destroy it.

WORK WITH A YOUNG PERSON. Remember that as adults, we are role models for our students and children. With the increasing number of daily commitments, it is understandable that many adults are pressed for time. However, if there is a way to become involved in a volunteer activity along with the young people in your life, do it. Not only are you "practicing what you preach," but you are also spending time in yet another positive way, not just when special events arise. After you have worked together to help some-one else, you have a basis for discussing important issues related to value systems, aging or illness, social change, how and why people help each other, how it feels to need someone's help, and how to implement change. Both of you will learn and grow from your experiences. That interdependence will also build a sense of teamwork.

TEACH THEM TO BE POSITIVE WITH THEIR PEERS AND FAMILY.

Several years ago we learned a strategy that helps our families when they become negative or begin to have lots of arguments. First, we sit down and discuss the situation and acknowledge that we are having some problems. Then we promise to say or do three nice things in the next twenty-four hour period. The next day, we get together and share our positive words and actions. We also compliment each other for the nice things that were done directly on our behalf. The key here is to start a positive cycle. What people say or do doesn't matter as much as the fact that they are starting a habit of positive actions. Contributions include even the smallest comments or actions, such as:

- ☼ Listening when a friend at school needs to talk.

- ☼ Getting a cold drink for someone without being asked.

- ☼ Offering to help a teacher return materials to the library.

- ☼ Giving a younger sibling a ride to the mall.

- ☼ Letting someone who's in a hurry go first in the checkout line.

☀ Calling a grandparent to say hello.

☀ Holding the door for the student with a broken ankle.

☀ Unloading the dishwasher without being told.

☀ Complimenting a friend on his or her haircut.

We repeat this for as long as it takes to get back on track with people. Pretty soon, people start to notice the nice things we've done and we get thanks, praise, smiles, and even hugs. It is a simple way to start to remember that we are good people whom others like and respect.

HELP THEM SEE THAT THEY ARE POSITIVE ROLE MODELS, TOO.

Many adolescents and teenagers respond more to influence from peers than pressure from family. Students with great leadership ability may sometimes use that ability to lead their peers into unproductive, illegal, or even dangerous activities. If you can identify the young people who have strong leadership skills and start to give them prosocial responsibilities, they can have a profound effect on others. When our young leaders are asked to do things like organizing a tutoring program, leading a drive to collect sneakers for homeless children, or painting murals instead of graffiti, many will respond in effective ways. Not only will they retain their position of leadership, but their peers may also follow them into more positive pursuits. So, when you identify the young person who has been the "ringleader," you may have identified a potential ally. By appealing to the young person's intelligence, power, and sense of responsibility, you can sometimes channel his or her energy into activities that will benefit everyone.

"I believe to the depth of my heart that a teenager who has spent a few hours a week helping a younger child learn to read, or spent a few hours at a hospice helping an older person reach the end of their life in dignity, is a changed person."

—General Colin L. Powell, United States Army (retired)
Secretary of State (2001-)

http://63.98.236.133/FivePromises/otgb.cfm

MY REFLECTIONS

WEBSITES/RESOURCES

- www.usinfo.state.gov/usa/volunteer (U.S. Department of State-Volunteerism in the U.S.)
- www.bygpub.com/books/tg2rw/volunteer.htm (The Teenager's Guide to the Real World Online)
- www.top100familysites.com (Top 100 Family Sites)

REFERENCES

Apter, Terri. *The confident child: Raising a child to try, learn, and care.* W. W. Norton, 1997.

Baldrige, Letitia. *Letitia Baldrige's more than manners!: Raising today's kids to have kind manners and good hearts.* Scribner, 1997.

Karnes, Frances A., Suzanne M. Bean, and Rosemary Wallner. *Girls and young women leading the way: 20 true stories about leadership.* Free Spirit Publishing, 1993.

NOTES TO MYSELF

IDEA 11

MONITOR THEIR BEHAVIOR

"The message brought to me was simple and can be projected by any parent: it is not the way your child looks or how cool they can act, but their own standards and determination which lead to success. These are the determining factors for my future."

—Leslie, 15

PAY ATTENTION TO THEIR FRIENDS. You can learn a lot about young people by paying attention to the people with whom they like to spend time. Because young people often are easily influenced by their peers, it is very important to get to know their friends. When you notice that a young person is having a strong negative influence on one of your children or students, address this issue. If there is something about a young person that makes you uncomfortable, suspicious, or nervous, pay attention to that feeling. Try to analyze exactly what about the person bothers you. The ways young people dress, style their hair, talk, walk, and treat each other are important clues. While expressing individuality is a normal part of growing up, certain patterns of behavior are indicators that students may be alienated, involved in drug use or gangs, or seriously depressed.

When you, as a parent or teacher, see behaviors that prompt concern, you should address them and discuss them. Many adults don't always take the time or have the energy to deal with minor issues. However, if you ignore small problems long enough, you may find yourself facing larger, more complex problems. When addressing these issues, proceed with caution. If you do identify a young person whose influence is a problem, think before you act.

Forbidding your child to see his friend or telling a student to avoid her friend might have just the opposite effect, that is, the two may become even closer friends in defiance of your demands. Before you overreact, try talking calmly, which means both listening and asking questions.

IF YOU FEEL THERE'S A PROBLEM, LOOK AT YOUR OWN CHILD. We have both been lucky in that our children have usually had wonderful friends. Sometimes, though, they have associated with individuals about whom we had some concerns. This seemed to occur during times when they were experiencing difficulties of their own. They chose friends who were experiencing similar difficulties. When we are most unhappy and struggling hardest to find our way, we need lots of positive support. Unfortunately, if we are spending time with unhappy, struggling friends who cannot provide that support, things may get worse as they draw us deeper into feelings of depression, anger, or frustration. Keeping in mind that your goal as a responsible adult is to support the young person you know, instead of focusing on how to end particular relationships, try taking some positive steps to strengthen your bonds with your child or student.

- ☼ Spend more time together.

- ☼ Find some time to talk about how things are going.

- ☼ Check to see if grades are slipping, especially in more than one class. If so, ask the student what's going on. Offer to help.

- ☼ Let them know that you are going to check up on where they go and what they do. (Nothing too embarrassing here, perhaps just a phone call to other parents or waiting up to say "hi" after an evening out.)

- ☼ Let them know you care. Tell them how important they are to you.

- ☼ Suggest that they include at least one other, more acceptable friend in some activities. Don't let them see only one person or small group all of the time.

- ☼ Tell them your concerns honestly. When you do this, explain that you care about them and don't want them to get hurt. Remind them that part of your job as a teacher or parent is to guide them and keep them from harm whenever possible.

- ☼ Keep tabs on where they are and who they are with. Require that they keep in touch with you, especially at nights and on the weekend. Close supervision works!

☼ Seek professional help if you can. Sometimes a change in friends and a pattern of troublesome behavior is indicative of some strong feelings that might best be dealt with by a licensed professional counselor.

SPEND TIME WITH THEIR FRIENDS, TOO. We already have discussed the need to spend time with the young people in your life. By extending the time you spend to their friends and acquaintances, you have an opportunity to gather more information before you make a judgment about another young person's character. Invite them to your home. Include them in a family dinner. Allow them to spend the night. Many children and teenagers know exactly how to "snow" adults. They have figured out just what to say and do to impress teachers and parents. However, the more time you spend together, the more likely it is that you will get to know them well enough to decide what's real and what's fake. It is also possible that you can have a positive effect on a young person who needs a little supervision and guidance.

CONSIDER YOUR OPTIONS IF A PROBLEM GETS SERIOUS. There are many youth today who have serious emotional and behavioral problems. Some of these problems, like substance abuse and suicide, are extremely

dangerous. If you believe that a young person you know is having serious difficulty, carefully consider several alternatives:

- ☀ Consider talking to the parents of the young person who is having problems. Do not be accusatory. If you can share your concerns in a calm, nonjudgmental way, the parents can take it from there.

- ☀ Consider asking another student to talk to his or her friend who is having problems. Again, with this age group, peers are often more influential than adults. A troubled youth might listen to someone his or her own age.

- ☀ Consider talking to the guidance counselor at school. If you think that confidentiality can be maintained, discuss the problem with the student's counselor. The counselor might be able to arrange to call the student in for a conversation and get a sense of how things are going.

- ☀ Consider telling the young person what you suspect. Offer to help or to get help. Explain that your only purpose is to offer assistance, not to get him or her in trouble. Ask if he or she would like your help.

- ☀ If you suspect abuse or potential suicide, you have no choice but to act quickly within the guidelines of the law and your school district's policies.

"If your child asks a specific drug-related question you can't answer, make that an excuse for a trip to the library or a dip into the Internet. The more accurate information children have, the less vulnerable they are to half-baked theories about what's cool and what's not."

—Betsy Van Dorn

"Laying the Foundation"
http://familyeducation.com/article/0,1120,3-373,00.html

MY REFLECTIONS

WEBSITES/RESOURCES

- www.drugfreeamerica.org (Partnership For a Drug-Free America)
- www.health.org (Substance Abuse and Mental Health Services Administration; PREVLINE-Prevention Online)
- www.effectivediscipline.com (Effective Discipline)

REFERENCES

Edwards, C. Drew. *How to handle a hard-to-handle kid*. Free Spirit Publishing, 1999.

Giannetti, Charlene C. and Margaret Sagarese. *Parenting 911: How to safeguard and rescue your 10- to 15-year-old from substance abuse, sexual encounters...and other risky situations*. Broadway Books, 1999.

Turecki, Stanley and Sarah Wernick. *Normal children have problems, too: How parents can understand and help*. Bantam Doubleday Dell, 1995.

NOTES TO MYSELF

_____

_____

_____

_____

_____

_____

_____

_____

_____

_____

_____

_____

IDEA 12

TEACH THEM SELF-RELIANCE

"So you change your expectations, you expect more from yourself and less from others. You begin to understand that if you don't do it yourself, no one else is going to do it for you."

—Ken, 16

SET REASONABLE LIMITS, THEN GIVE THEM CHOICES. One way to avoid problems of control with teenagers is to set limits that are reasonable and then be consistent in enforcing them. In the process of doing this, give young people choices and options, so that they don't feel like you're always "telling them what to do." For example:

☼ When setting a curfew for your fifteen-year-old son, you might explain that you feel most comfortable with an 11:30 weekend curfew most of the time. However, once a month you would be willing to extend that time to 12:00 or 12:30 if there were a special occasion. Your son can choose when he wants to use his late-night privileges, as long as he tells you ahead of time. If he's late on the regular nights, he loses the next month's late night.

☼ If you are a secondary school teacher, when you structure your next instructional unit, plan on a set of basic requirements. Then allow students to choose one assignment from a list of three options for the final ten to fifteen percent of their grades. Give choices.

☼ When assigning young people to help clean up, either in school or at home, let them alternate jobs so no one gets stuck doing the same thing all of the time. Draw names to see who picks first at the beginning of the year, then take turns.

- ☀ When asking your son or daughter to help with mowing the yard, give him or her a deadline of Saturday at 5:00. Don't nag. Mowing any time during the week is okay, but if he or she misses the deadline, he or she also misses Saturday evening out with friends.

- ☀ Negotiate, negotiate, negotiate. Whenever possible, sit down with the young people in your life and discuss decisions together. This doesn't mean you always give in and let them have their way. It does mean you should be reasonable and listen to their side of the story. With a little give and take, everyone can end up feeling okay about rules and responsibilities.

TEACH THEM TO MANAGE THEIR OWN MONEY. One universal truth about teenagers and children is that they can spend money! Arguments about money are a frequent source of conflict in many families. Rather than get embroiled in constant bickering about finances with your child, set up a plan and be consistent. The plan you set up should be one that is unique to your situation. No two families have exactly the same income, expenses, structure, values, or beliefs about allowance, spending money, or who pays for what. Sit down with your children and set up a system that works for you. It should address these points:

- ☀ Is money given freely or is it earned?

- ☀ How much money is allotted to each young person?

- ☀ What is each child expected to pay for with his or her own money?

- ☀ Is there a requirement that a portion of each person's money go to savings, charity, or other accounts?

- ☀ When the young person has a car or access to a car, who is responsible for gas, repairs, and insurance?

- ☀ What are the rules about borrowing and lending?

Young people should be encouraged to earn some money of their own and then be allowed to make their own choices about how to spend it. This means that even when you know they're making a foolish purchase, sometimes you let them do it anyway. This also means that if they spend all their money on video games on Saturday and they don't have any for the movies on Sunday, you say, "Oh, well," and let them figure it out for themselves. If the pattern continues, then a more direct teaching lesson is in order and some limits might need to be set. There are also times when children want extravagant items of clothing or sports equipment. Instead of paying for everything, you could agree to pay the amount that a basic item would cost and let them make up the difference. Parents can still provide guidance and encourage good habits by doing things like matching the amount children save. Teaching children to manage money is an important step toward eventual independence and self-reliance.

DON'T DO EVERYTHING FOR THEM. It's amazing to see college students who can't balance a checkbook. It is even more surprising when we see adults who don't know how to do their own laundry or expect others to pick up after them. If you want your students or children to do things for themselves, then you have to start expecting and requiring that they do so. They need some practice. This means you have to be willing to let them do some things differently from the way you might do them. It also means that you might have to wait while they learn how to do things. However, the sooner you begin the process, the sooner you get results. Even very young children can do simple, easy tasks, then work up to more complicated jobs. Getting them to help also takes the burden off of you to do everything and might leave you more time to have some fun! At school, it is important that teenage students take responsibility for keeping an assignment book, getting homework in on time, and completing long-range assignments. If you constantly nag or call parents, sometimes students will fail to assume responsibility for their own actions.

MY REFLECTIONS

WEBSITES/RESOURCES

- www.childslife.com (Childs Life)
- www.parenthoodweb.com (Parenthood.com)

REFERENCES

Bloch, Douglas, and Jon Merritt. *Positive self-talk for children: Teaching self-esteem through affirmations: A guide for parents, teachers & counselors.* Bantam Doubleday Dell, 1993.

Shellenberger, Susie, and Greg Johnson. *Cars, curfews, parties, and parents . . . (77 pretty important ideas).* Bethany House, 1995.

Otfinoski, Steve. *The kid's guide to money: Earning it, saving it, spending it, growing it, sharing it.* Scholastic, 1996.

NOTES TO MYSELF

IDEA 13 — FOCUS ON SOCIAL LEARNING

"So once again you are out in the world but now with great expectations for yourself. What if you fail? What if no one ever notices you and your struggles?"

—Lisa, 13

HELP THEM SEE THAT SOCIAL SKILLS ARE IMPORTANT. Time and time again in life we encounter people who are very bright or very well educated, yet aren't as successful as they would like to be. Sometimes, their lack of success is due to a lack of social skills. Social skills include interpersonal abilities like making and keeping friends, compromising, apologizing, or controlling impulsivity. Social skills can also involve the abilities necessary to handle our strong feelings, like anger, frustration, or depression. We also need social skills that involve taking responsibility for our own actions, like decision making, problem solving, or goal setting. Schools have always focused on academic learning. However, it seems that in today's world, teaching academic skills is not enough. For children who haven't learned social skills at home or who are so alienated that they don't see a need to use their social skills, schools must be more responsive. The real world of work, families, friendships, and neighborhoods demands a lot more than academic or vocational training. Teachers and parents have some say in the curricula of public schools. It is important to recognize the need for our students to learn social skills and to ask that our schools teach them. At home, too, all of us need to be teachers. By example, by direct instruction, and by structuring situations made for practice, we can help students see that to succeed in the world, they must get along with others. It is in their best interest to gain skills that will help them relate successfully to others and to meet society's expectations.

BE CLEAR AND SPECIFIC. Often, adults make a lot of assumptions about young people. Because our young people are often bright, mature, and seem very knowledgeable or even sophisticated, we assume that they automatically know how to do things. Getting along with people is probably the most complicated task in the world. It requires that we observe and process information very quickly, make rapid decisions, constantly adjust and modify behavior to fit different individuals and situations, and see things from someone else's perspective. All of these actions require high-level thinking and creative responses. Fourteen- and fifteen-year olds may not be able to figure out all of these steps without adult assistance. In addition, if we haven't been good role models, then the young person may have difficulty visualizing what it is that he or she needs to do. So, it is important to teach our young people positive ways to act and react. For example:

☀ If your daughter has had a run-in with a teacher, help her figure out when and how to apologize. (Go in to school early, before the other kids are there. Start by saying, "Mr. Smith, do you have a minute to talk to me about what happened yesterday? Thanks. I just wanted to tell you that I'm sorry. I was upset and I got carried away.") With some kids, we need to help them practice very specifically the actual words to say so they don't feel awkward or phony.

☀ When two students in your class have resorted to name calling during a disagreement, you might need to step in and teach them how to negotiate. Negotiation is a very high-level skill that involves careful listening, calm suggestions, turn taking, and decision making. It may be that before you start a group activity, you always write down steps for them to follow and rules that must be agreed upon. Then give them a simulated situation, have them take opposite sides, and let them practice.

☀ When young people start part-time jobs, they have an opportunity to practice lots of positive skills (like listening calmly to complaints, apologizing, expressing a legitimate concern, smiling even when they feel terrible, and recognizing volatile situations). Help them before they start working by discussing hypothetical situations or by talking about some good and bad experiences you have had as a consumer. Pair them up and let them role play difficult scenarios from real life situations.

Smiling Is Important to Everyone

SMILE AND HAVE FUN. One of the nicest things you can do for children is teach them how to enjoy themselves, especially how to see the humor in situations and to share that humor with others. As a start, teach the young people in your life to smile. Encourage them to smile when they meet someone, to smile and say hello when they pass adults in the hall, to smile at a customer when they start to work, to smile at each other when they're in class, and to smile when saying goodbye. If a young person hasn't been used to smiling and begins to smile a lot, he or she will start to get results from others almost immediately. After they have become comfortable with smiling, start to encourage them to share jokes and laughter. Laughter seems to have positive physical as well as psychological benefits for people and, if nothing else, is just plain fun. For some children, life hasn't been very funny, and adults will need to teach them to appreciate and use humor in the same way they are taught to appreciate and use language or music.

When helping young people learn about humor, use cartoons from the newspaper, stories written in magazines, funny photos that capture spur-of-the-moment events, and even joke books. You may also need to teach the difference between laughing with and laughing at. All of us want to have a positive influence on our environment, and sharing enjoyment is a nice way to begin. However, our enjoyment should not come at someone else's expense.

"Bullying is something most children encounter in one form or another. Children struggle with being called names, being picked upon, being excluded, not knowing how to make friends, or being the ones acting unkindly or aggressively toward others. All forms of bullying are abusive and all are opportunities to teach children how to get along, how to be considerate people, how to be part of a community or group."

—Sherryll Kraizer, Ph.D.

"Dealing with Bullies," About.com
http://canadateachers.about.com/library/b/bully.htm

MY REFLECTIONS

WEBSITES/RESOURCES

- www.ed.gov/pubs/parents (Publications for Parents)
- www.nncc.org (National Network for Child Care)
- www.wheres-daddy.com (Where's Daddy?)

REFERENCES

Eyre, Linda, and Richard M. Eyre. *Teaching your child responsibility*. Fireside, 1994.

Giannetti, Charlene C., and Margaret Sagarese. *Cliques: 8 steps to help your child survive the social jungle*. Broadway Books, 2001.

Lewis, Barbara A., Pamela Espeland, and Caryn Perny. *The kid's guide to social action: How to solve the social problems you choose—and turn creative thinking into positive action*. Free Spirit Publishing, 1998.

NOTES TO MYSELF

IDEA 14 · ACCEPT THEM FOR WHO THEY ARE

"Parents should judge kids by their efforts and ability and not by how they dress."

—Cyndy, 12

REMEMBER THAT NO ONE IS PERFECT. Sometimes grown-ups want children and teenagers to act like adults, only better. They want perfection. There are all kinds of parents and teachers who want perfect children for all kinds of reasons. They want perfectly behaved children so that they look good to family, friends, and fellow educators. They want perfect athletes so that their team will win a championship. They want all A's and no B's because they see their child's or student's grades as a reflection of their own intelligence or teaching ability. They want the best, all of the time and in all types of situations. Guess what! Their children pressure themselves to be perfect, too. They try to fit in with a popular crowd, to be cute or handsome, to hit home runs, to be a soloist in the choir, and to get a 4.00 grade point average. Don't misunderstand. High expectations are not inherently bad or damaging or even overwhelming for young people. However, when the expectations that parents and teachers hold for children are unrealistic or are not in line with the youth's abilities or interests, there can be problems.

One problem has to do with self-esteem and can be a long-term issue for many individuals. If we think of self-esteem as the result of the match between the goals we set and what we actually achieve, then we can see the potential problems. When we set goals that are too low, we never challenge ourselves and may end up unfulfilled and feeling like we wasted our time.

Expectations Should Match a Child's Abilities and Interests

If we set goals that are too high, we may never reach them, and we may end
up feeling like failures or that we're not good enough, despite the fact that
our achievements might really be significant and worthwhile. Many very
bright kids are perfectionists. They can't finish anything, because it might not
be perfect or they can't take pleasure in finishing anything because they're
always looking for something else to go after next. Sometimes, children end
up using alcohol, drugs, sex, or engaging in other risk-taking behaviors to ease

the pressure. Before you push too hard, take a good long look at yourself to see why you're pushing. If it has more to do with you than with them, stop.

ENJOY THEIR DIFFERENCES. When you spend time around children, you soon find out that no two of them are alike. There are some young people who will make you laugh, some who are interested in deep, philosophical conversations, and others with whom you will enjoy spending quiet time. If you're lucky, when you are a teacher or parent you will have an opportunity to get to know many of your students, children, and children's friends. When you do get to find out how different they are, it's important that you try to enjoy their differences, instead of expecting each of them to be a straight A student or a varsity athlete. As adults, we know from experience that it's no fun to be forced into a mold and expected to be just like everyone else. Children are just like we are; they want to be allowed to be themselves, too. Valuing our differences and appreciating the unique characteristics each individual has will enrich our lives! Variety in people, just like variety in activities, prevents boredom and keeps us young.

LET THEM KNOW YOU LIKE THEM. When we feel that someone likes us, it's a lot easier to relax and be nice. We are more inclined to be open, honest, and pleasant. There are many ways to show kids that you like them, many of which we have already mentioned. Here are some of the most important:

☼ **Tell Them**

"I really like being with you."

☼ **Compliment Their Unique Skills**

"You sure are patient with your younger brother."

☼ **Spend Time**

"Why don't we rent a video tonight and watch it together?"

☼ **Use Body Language**

Smile, give them a pat on the shoulder, or greet them with a high five.

☼ **Give Them Freedom (Before They Ask)**

"You have really been responsible at your job. Maybe you'd like a later curfew tonight."

☼ **Give Them Responsibility**

"It would help me so much if you could handle recording these grades. Would you mind?"

☼ **Laugh Together**

"Wait until you hear about our dog. It was so funny!"

☼ **Praise Them When You Know They Can Hear**

"Boy, you wouldn't believe the way Susie has been treating people lately. She has gone out of her way to help the new kids. I'm so proud of her!"

☼ **Include Them When You Go Places**

"Dad and I were wondering if you would like to get Mexican food with us tonight. You can choose the restaurant."

"Perfectionism and uncommon physical characteristics can effect a child's self-esteem negatively; parents should be realistic in their expectations and they should redefine their children's characteristics in positive terms to help counter the negative effects."

—K. H. Kim, *Therapeutic Parenting*

MY REFLECTIONS

WEBSITES/RESOURCES

- www.connectforkids.org (Connect for Kids: Guidance for Grownups)
- www.youthdevelopment.org (Institute for Youth Development)

REFERENCES

Adderholdt-Elliott, Miriam, and Jan Goldberg. *Perfectionism: What's bad about being too good?* Free Spirit Publishing, 1999.

Popov, Linda Kavelin, Dan Popov, and John Kavelin. *The family virtues guide: Simple ways to bring out the best in our children and ourselves.* Plume, 1997.

Salt, J. S. *Always accept me for who I am.* Three Rivers Press, 1999.

NOTES TO MYSELF

IDEA 15 GET HELP WHEN YOU NEED IT

"I always feel rushed. There are never enough hours to get everything done. Something always stands in my way. I have to do everything right the first TIME."

—Mimi, 15

DON'T BE AFRAID TO ASK FOR HELP. At various times in our lives, we all need help. As teachers or parents of young people, we face numerous pressures and problems. Many situations are so serious or dangerous that we cannot deal with them alone. When those situations arise, it is important to ask for help. There are some adults who feel that they should be able to handle everything by themselves and who think that to do less is a sign of weakness or failure. We believe that the opposite is true, that it takes great courage and strength to ask for help. It requires that we be honest with others and ourselves and that we face our problems head on, without trying to avoid and ignore them. The following situations are some that you may need to seek help in resolving:

- ☼ When a student or child expresses feelings of hopelessness that you think might indicate a possibility of suicide

- ☼ When you suspect that a student or other young person is a victim of abuse or neglect. (The law says that you must intervene here.)

- ☼ When you have knowledge that a crime has been committed

- ☼ When a young person shows signs of a drug or alcohol problem

- ☼ When your child or student experiences sudden, noticeable changes in eating or sleeping patterns

- ☼ When the youth is aggressive, explosive, or threatening to himself/herself or others

☀ When your child or student undergoes sudden or marked changes in appearance or dress

☀ When the young person changes peer groups and the new friends make you feel uncomfortable

☀ When the young person's grades in school fall or when she or he drops out of normal activities

☀ When there are long periods of overt hostility to the point that you wonder if things will ever get better

☀ When you start to so strongly dislike a particular child or student that you cannot be nice to him or her

☀ When you feel like you need help, for any reason

The list above includes some examples of when to exercise basic, common sense in seeking assistance. Unless you are prone to overreaction, if you think you need help, you probably do. The next list includes individuals or groups from whom you can get the help you need. Different situations require different responses. If the problems you and a young person face are serious, in terms of physical danger or legal responsibility, of course the help you get must address those issues. For other less serious problems, there are lots of people who can and will help:

☀ the school counselor

☀ the district's behavior specialist

☀ your school district's crisis counselor

☀ your local mental health agency

☀ the state or local division of child protective services

☀ a mental health clinic

☀ private or public family counselors

☀ psychotherapists and psychiatrists

☀ your priest, pastor, or minister; or a youth director at your church or synagogue

☀ support groups for parents of kids in trouble

- private or public agencies who deal specifically with children and youth

- private and public psychiatric hospitals

- drug and alcohol abuse or runaway hotlines

- another adult, perhaps a parent or teacher whom you trust

- the police department's youth liaison

- one of the young person's friends, or perhaps a friend who knows there's trouble

- other parents or teachers who may already have experienced some of the problems you're having

"You can't personally transform the whole world from a violent place into one where peace and gentleness reign supreme; you can, however, make your own home a peaceful, gentle place. And the most crucial way to do so is to foster your child's self-esteem."

—Aleta Koman, M.Ed., *The Parenting Survival Kit*

MY REFLECTIONS

_____

_____

_____

_____

_____

_____

_____

_____

_____

_____

_____

_____

_____

WEBSITES/RESOURCES

- www.youthchg.com (Youth Change: Your Problem-Kid Problem-Solver)
- www.jedfoundation.org (The Jed Foundation)

REFERENCES

Elium, Jeanne, and Don Elium. *Raising a teenager: Parents and the nurturing of a responsible teen.* Celestial Arts, 1999.

Karres, Erika V. Shearin. *Violence proof your kids now: How to recognize the 8 warning signs and what to do about them.* Conari Press, 2000.

Koman, Aleta, and Edward Myers. *The parenting survival kit.* Perigree, 2000.

NOTES TO MYSELF

SUMMARY

You have just read 15 ideas for working with today's youth. These ideas are a place to start when relating to young people at home and at school. However, because of the serious nature of the problems we have with our children and students, it is important to consider lots of different ideas, not just these 15. While some might work for you and the children you know, others may not be helpful at all. That's okay. The important thing is to get lots of ideas and keep trying them until something you do makes a difference.

The efforts you make to help a young person are important. The assistance we provide to today's young people who are alienated, hopeless, angry, and uninvolved in our value system will help shape our society and have an impact on our lifestyles and relationships. It is critical that we not give up on the young people who are hard to like and harder to control, the ones who push us away and refuse to accept our attention. They need us the most, and we must try to make a difference in their lives.

OTHER PUBLICATIONS OF INTEREST FROM SOPRIS WEST

DISCOVERY INSTITUTE

Eric Larsen, M.Ed.

Grades 6-12

This proven-successful program teaches positive social skills to middle and high school students from a student-centered and skill-based approach. Learn to engage students' attention and create positive change by implementing direct instruction, modeling, role-playing, experiential activities, and more. Critical skills are presented in six sequential units: effective group skills and team building, anger management, transactional communication, assertiveness training, problem solving, and conflict resolution.

Program training, which provides the skills needed to effectively implement the program, is available in three formats: (1) on-site training at your school district or school; (2) seminars in Colorado; or (3) the Video Instruction Series (13 videotapes, ten Video Series Workbooks, and one Teacher Training Workbook). On-site training, which includes the Video Instruction Series at a reduced price, is the recommended format for successful implementation.

KIDS WHO OUTWIT ADULTS

by John R. Seita, Ed.D. and Larry K. Brendtro, Ph.D.

Grades 6-12

Strength-Based Interventions for Your Toughest Kids

—From Starr Commonwealth

In *Kids Who Outwit Adults*, authors Seita and Brendtro disclose the "private logic" behind kids' violent and defiant acts. Weaving together an effective, highly rewarding approach based on tried-and-true resilience models, insights from their years of experience working with youths, and youths' own heart wrenching accounts, the authors illuminate the internal strengths and external supports kids need in order to break out of these negative behavior patterns. Seita and Brendtro are your guides through the deeper world of youth scare tactics and coping mechanisms.　Product code: 160OUT

NO DISPOSABLE KIDS

by Larry Brendtro, Ph.D.; Arlin Ness, ACSW, LLD; and Martin Mitchell, Ed.D.
Grades: 1-12

This book—based on the authors' groundbreaking work at Starr Commonwealth with court-ordered youths—challenges the notion of any child being "too far gone" to be helped. The authors provide profound insight into the world of these youths, not only sharing strategies drawn from the best of the resiliency models (including the CCDO, Circle of Courage, and Re-ED), but also illustrating their successful use with actual cases. By reframing rebellious acts as signs of resilience, the authors uncover the natural self-righting tendencies of youths who are progressing toward normal adult development, despite adverse circumstances.

TO ORDER ANY OF THESE TITLES, OR FOR MORE INFORMATION, CONTACT

SOPRIS
WEST

(800) 547-6747

Fax: (303) 776-5934

www.sopriswest.com